POSITIVE STEPS

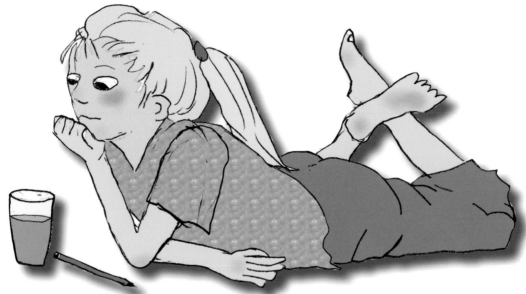

Being Honest

by Susan Martineau

with illustrations by Hel James

A⁺

Smart Apple Media

Published by Smart Apple Media
P.O. Box 3263, Mankato, Minnesota 56002

Printed in the United States of America at Corporate Graphics, in North Mankato, Minnesota.

Library of Congress Cataloging-in-Publication Data
Martineau, Susan.
  Being honest / by Susan Martineau ; with illustrations by Hel James.
     p. cm. — (Positive steps)
  Includes index.
  ISBN 978-1-59920-489-5 (library binding)
  1. Honesty—Juvenile literature. I. Title.
  BJ1533.H7M38 2012
  179'.9—dc22

                                           2010046933

Created by Appleseed Editions, Ltd.
Well House, Friars Hill, Guestling,
Designed and illustrated by Hel James
Edited by Mary-Jane Wilkins
Picture research by Su Alexander

Picture credits
Contents page Yuri Arcurs/Shutterstock; 4t Orange Line Media/Shutterstock, b StockLite/ Shutterstock; 6-7 background Selyutina Olga/Shutterstock; 8-9 background Yoyo_sic/Shutterstock; 11t Wavebreakmedia Ltd/Shutterstock, b Zulufoto/Shutterstock; 12-13 background Lakov Kalinin/ Shutterstock; 14-15 background Hel James, 15 Bronwyn Photo/Shutterstock; 17 Photoroller/ Shutterstock; 18 background Alexander Chaikin/Shutterstock, Angelo Giampiccolo/Shutterstock; 19 Paulaphoto/Shutterstock; 20 StockLite/Shutterstock; 21 Rob Marmion/Shutterstock; 24 background Rob Byron/Shutterstock; 25 Mandy Godbehear/Shutterstock; 26-27 background Jan Kratochvila/ Shutterstock, 27 Losevsky Pavel/Shutterstock; 28-29 background Lakov Kalinin/Shutterstock; 32 Wavebreakmedia Ltd/Shutterstock
Cover: Wavebreakmedia Ltd/Shutterstock

DAD0048
3-2011

9 8 7 6 5 4 3 2 1

Contents

Tell the truth.

Let's Be Honest

Being **honest** helps people to get along with each other. It stops us from doing or saying things that might hurt someone else. If we are honest, other people will be able to **trust** us.

Don't be a tattletale.

LET'S TALK ABOUT . . .

Read out loud the things these children are saying. What do you think happened to make them say these things? Are these children and their friends being honest?

Stop copying my work!

4

What can you do?
Your friends, family, and teachers will know what to expect from you if you behave honestly. This book shows you lots of different ways of being honest.

Telling the Truth

When we tell the **truth** we are being honest. Sometimes it is not very easy to tell the truth because you think you might get into trouble. Telling **lies** is **dishonest**.

People usually find out when we lie to them. This will upset them. They might not trust us or believe what we say anymore.

Harry, did you break that window?

No, it was Ali.

LET'S TALK ABOUT . . .

Harry did break the window. What do you think will happen when the person Harry has lied to finds out that it was him and not Ali? Do you think they might be even more angry with Harry for telling lies?

Owning Up

Try to think of words Harry could use to **own up** about breaking the window. Here are some ideas.

I'm afraid I did it.

Please don't be mad, but it was me.

I am sorry. It was me.

Saying You're Sorry

If we hurt someone or break something, we should always say sorry. We need to be honest about it and **apologize**, even if it was an accident.

I didn't mean to hurt you. I'm really sorry.

We should always try to say sorry as soon as we can. Also, if someone says sorry to us, we should accept their apology.

It's OK.

What can you do?

- When you are saying sorry it is important to look at the person. Show them you *really* mean it.

- Don't just run off as soon as you've apologized. Make sure the person has accepted your apology and that they are not upset anymore.

Time to Say Sorry!

Practice saying sorry. You can do this with a friend or even in front of the mirror! Think about the words you might say.

I didn't mean to be rude.

Are you OK?

Can I help fix it?

I'm *really* sorry.

It's a Secret

Mina has been asked to keep a secret. She's writing to a friend from her old school. She's worried and not sure what to do.

Hi Alice,

My new school is OK. I miss you though. There's another new girl here named Charlie. Some of the girls pick on her but she's told me not to tell. I don't want to be a tattletale but they're being really mean.

Write soon,

Love from Mina

XOXO

Let's talk about . . .

What do you think Mina should do? Secrets like these are not good secrets. They hurt people, and Mina will not be a tattletale if she talks to someone about it. Perhaps she could ask Charlie if she can go with her to ask for help from someone older or a teacher.

Good and Bad Secrets

Take a look at these secrets and decide if it is more honest to tell someone the truth or to keep the secret.

My best friend isn't really sick. He doesn't want to go to school.

My mom is having a secret surprise party for a friend.

I saw Kaya take something out of Emily's bag.

Trusting Our Friends

Oh, get away from Ella. She smells.

Our friends should be honest with us. We need to be able to trust our friends.

Sherri is sometimes very friendly to Ella. But at other times she ignores her on the playground and even says unkind things behind her back.

I thought she was my friend . . .

Is Sherri an honest or fake friend? Would you trust her? Friends who say things behind our backs are not very **loyal**.

Honest or Fake?

Take a look at these phrases. Maybe say them out loud. Decide which ones are about honest friends and which are about **fake** friends.

Leave you out of games

Are loyal

Spread lies about you

Apologize if they've hurt you

Are kind to you

Take your things without asking you

 **LET'S TALK ABOUT . . .**

Do you think it is all right to tell white lies sometimes? Can you think of any you have told? If it feels wrong to lie, then the lie is probably not a white lie.

Tell the Truth? Would you tell the truth or a white lie here?

You do not like the present your grandma has just given you.

Your friend has to wear glasses and thinks they look awful.

I can't find it anywhere.

You have lost the new watch your dad bought you.

Stop Cheating!

Playing games is lots of fun. We play them at school with friends or at home with our family. But they are only fun if everyone follows the rules.

It's my turn!

No, it's not. Stop cheating!

I'm not playing with you anymore.

Playing games with people who **cheat** is not much fun. Cheating is a bit like lying. It is not very honest and makes everyone angry.

What can you do?

- Make sure that everyone knows the rules of the game before you start.

- Don't shout and argue if you think someone has cheated.

- Tell the person that you can't trust them to play unless they behave honestly.

The Game Game

Play this game in class or with a group of friends. Everyone stands up. Take turns to say the name of a game or sport. If you can't think of one you have to sit down. The winner is the last one standing! No shouting or interrupting is allowed.

Chess

Monopoly

Hockey

Tennis

Go Fish

Football

Dominoes

Chutes and Ladders

Old Maid

Be Yourself

Ryan is friends with Matt, but he's not sure whether Matt is honest with him. Ryan misses his older sister who is away at college, and he writes to her about Matt.

Hi Sam,

Hope you're OK. There's a new boy at school named Matt. He's fun but I think he makes up stories. He says his dad is buying him a boat for his birthday. I like him, but I wish he would stop telling stupid lies.

Wish you were here,
Ryan

LET'S TALK ABOUT . . .

Do you believe Matt? Why might he make up stories? Have you ever said something you know isn't true to try to make yourself sound better than other people?

Just be yourself!

What can you do?

You will have more friends if you are just yourself. **Boasting** and **showing off** are not honest. Your friends might not trust you when they find out you have been **exaggerating**.

By being yourself you are being honest with yourself. This is just as important as being honest with other people.

19

Don't Copy!

Some lessons are harder than others. When we do not understand something, we might find it easier just to copy someone else's work.

Copying other people's work is really cheating and is not honest.

Stop looking at my work!

How do you feel if someone copies your work? Do you sometimes let them copy because you feel sorry for them or they say they won't be your friend if you don't let them?

Could you please explain it again?

What can you do?

If you don't understand something it is always best to ask the teacher to explain it again. Don't worry, you probably won't be the only one who is not sure. You are just being braver than the others when you ask to have it explained again.

Don't let other people copy your work. A true friend would not stop being your friend just because you say no.

Making Excuses

Sometimes we make **excuses** to try to get out of trouble. The problem is that excuses can cause more trouble! People can usually tell if we are making things up.

I'm late because the bus broke down.

Do you think these excuses are honest ones? Would you believe them?
It's always best to tell the truth so that when you really have a problem your parents, friends, and teachers will believe you and help you.

What can you do?

Take another look at the excuses. What would have been the best thing to say instead of making those excuses? For example, if you break something, just be honest and apologize instead of pretending it broke itself.

I'm sorry. I broke it.

It's Not Fair!

Sometimes a teacher might scold us for something we have not done. The teacher thinks it is our fault.

When no one else owns up or tells the teacher what really happened, we feel mad and upset.

Dan, why did you do that?

That's not fair! It wasn't me!

Look at these words. Do they describe how Dan might feel? Can you think of times when you have felt unfairly blamed for something you did not do?

sad

frustrated

angry

lonely

upset

What can you do?

- When other people let you take the blame, try not to lose your temper and shout, "It's not fair!"

- Instead, try to explain what really happened quietly and calmly. People are more likely to listen to you if you are polite.

That's Stealing!

Maria is staying with her cousin. They've been shopping with Maria's aunt and Maria writes to her friend Lauren about it.

Hi Lauren,

I'm having a good time at my aunt's. We all went shopping yesterday. It was OK, but my cousin dared me to **steal** a bag of candy! She said it didn't matter because it's only a small thing, but I feel really bad now.

I wish you were here.

Love, Maria

P.S. She told me not to tell anyone so please don't!

What would you say to Maria if you were Lauren? If you had been there would you have told her to put the candy back? Taking things without paying for them is stealing. It does not matter how small they are.

What can you do?

If a friend dares you to do something you know is wrong, it is important to stick up for what is right. Tell them you do not want to be dishonest.

A true friend would never force you to do something they know is wrong.

The stores are full of things we would like, but remember that stealing is against the law.

The Honest Choice

Being honest with your friends, family, and teachers is very important. This means telling the truth, being a loyal friend, and knowing when you should not keep a secret. Being honest with yourself is just as important.

Honest Words

Look back through the book and find the words in bold. Now write them down on a piece of paper in two lists. Make one list for words about being honest and another list for words about being dishonest.

The **bold** words are explained on pages 30–31.

Honest

own up
loyal

Dishonest

cheat
boast

Don't cheat or copy.

Glossary

apologize
to say you are sorry for something; to make an apology

boast
to say something that makes you sound better than other people

cheat
to break the rules of a game or trick someone

dishonest
not honest

exaggerate
to change stories about yourself or other people so that they sound better and more exciting than they really are

excuse
a way of explaining why you have done something wrong so that you will not get into trouble

fake
not true or honest

honest
not stealing, cheating, or telling lies

lie
to say something that you know
is not true or that you do not believe

loyal
being a true and honest friend

I'm sorry. I broke it.

own up

to tell the truth when you have done something wrong

show off

to try to make people think you are good at something or are better than you really are

steal

to take something that is not yours without paying for it or asking to borrow it

trust

to believe that someone is good and honest and would not hurt you

truth

what has really happened; to tell the truth is to say what is true.

Don't make things up.

Web Sites

It's My Life – PBS Kids: When Friends Fight
http://pbskids.org/itsmylife/friends/friendsfight/index.html

Kid's Health: Cheating
http://kidshealth.org/kid/feeling/emotion/cheating.html#cat20070

Kidsinco: Honesty
http://www.kidsinco.com/our-values/honesty/

Index

Tell the truth.